NATURAL WORLD

For a free color catalog describing Gareth Stevens' list of high-quality children's books call 1-800-433-0942.

Library of Congress Cataloging-in-Publication Data

Ganeri, Anita, 1961-
    Natural world / by Anita Ganeri and Moira Butterfield; illustrated by Peter Bull &
Paul Johnson.
      p. cm. -- (Fact finders)
      Bibliography: p.
      Includes index.
      Summary: Examines such aspects of the natural world as earth formations, weather, seas
and rivers, plants, and animals.
1. Natural history--Juvenile literature. [1. Natural history.] I. Butterfield, Moira, 1960- . II. Bull,
Peter (Peter T.), ill. III. Johnson, Paul, 1951- ill. IV. Title. V. Series.
QH48.G26   1989   508--dc20   89-11349
ISBN 0-8368-0133-4

This North American edition first published in 1989 by

Gareth Stevens Children's Books
7317 West Green Tree Road
Milwaukee, Wisconsin 53223, USA

Series editor: Rita Reitci
Research editor: Scott Enk

Printed in the United States of America

1 2 3 4 5 6 7 8 9 95 94 93 92 91 90 89

FACT FINDER

NATURAL WORLD

Written by A. Ganeri & M. Butterfield

Illustrated by P. Bull & P. Johnson

Gareth Stevens Children's Books
MILWAUKEE

THE NATURAL WORLD

This book is a wide-ranging introduction to the natural world around us. It includes lots of information about the Earth, from its physical shape to the animals and plants that live on it.

There are six chapters, each dealing with a different subject, explained below.

THE EARTH 6-11

In this section you can find out what materials make up the Earth and why earthquakes and eruptions occur on the Earth's surface. There's also information on how different types of rocks first formed, and you can find out about precious stones and fossils, too.

WEATHER 12-17

In this section you can see what causes the weather, for instance, why rain and snow fall and how clouds form. Dramatic weather, such as tornadoes, hurricanes, and monsoons, is explained. There are also some amazing weather facts and records, such as the biggest ever hailstones and the wettest place on Earth.

SEAS AND RIVERS 18-23

Over two-thirds of the Earth's surface lies under water, mostly salt water in the seas and oceans. This section is about the oceans and their currents and tides. You can also find out about how a river gradually grows from a small spring before flowing finally into the sea, and how water hollows out underground caves and forms ice sheets, glaciers, and icebergs.

PLANTS 24-31

This section looks at the varied world of plants, including the record breakers of the plant kingdom, such as the biggest flowers and trees. You can find out how plants make their own food, and why they have flowers. Some unusual plants are meat-eating and rock-eating plants.

ANIMALS 32-41

This section covers the main groups of animals: insects, fish, amphibians, reptiles, birds, and mammals. There are lots of amazing facts and records from the animal kingdom, too. For example, you can find out how far a kangaroo can leap and how much water a camel can drink at one time.

EARTH'S FUTURE 42-45

Many parts of the Earth are changing from industry or building. This can cause the destruction of animals and plants, and sometimes pollution that can even threaten human life. In this section you can find out about some of the Earth's pollution and conservation problems and how everyone can help to prevent them.

Each section in this book has a different colored strip across the top of its pages to make it easier for you to find and refer to. The colors are shown on the right.

THE EARTH

The Earth is part of the Solar System, a group of nine known planets traveling around the Sun. The Solar System is in a huge galaxy, or group of stars, called the Milky Way. The Milky Way has about 200 billion stars, of which the Sun is just one! In this section you can find out some basic facts about planet Earth.

The Earth is not completely round in shape. It bulges out slightly at the Equator and flattens out slightly at the Poles. It consists of four different layers of material, shown below.

The Earth's outer shell is called the crust. It is the thinnest of the four Earth layers, reaching about 25 miles (40 km) below the surface of the land at its thickest point.

The Earth's innermost core is a ball of metal about 1,500 miles (2,400 km) wide. Its heat may be about 45 times the temperature of boiling water!

Below the crust is the mantle, a thicker layer that may be up to 1,800 miles (2,900 km) thick, consisting of hot liquid rock.

The Earth has an outer core that is about 1,300 miles (2,100 km) thick. This outer core may be a mixture of very hot liquid iron and nickel.

One theory of the Earth's origin is that billions of years ago it condensed from clouds of gas, rock, and metal caused by an exploding star.

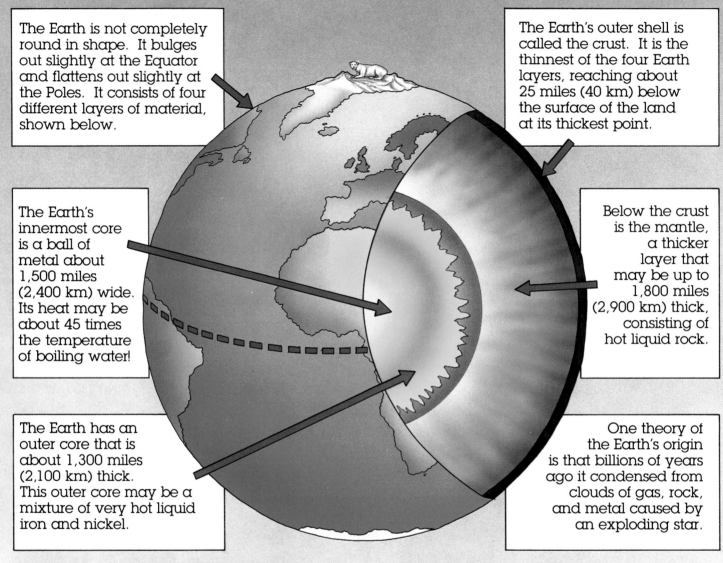

THE EARTH'S PLATES

The Earth's crust is broken into giant pieces called plates. They float on top of the mantle, moving very slowly.

When two plates collide with each other they cause cracks in the crust called fault lines. On the west coast of the United States, the San Andreas Fault runs for 600 miles (960 km). It resulted from two plates sliding slowly past each other.

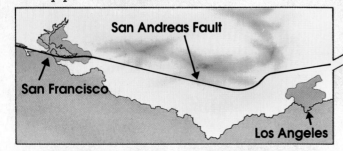

San Andreas Fault

San Francisco

Los Angeles

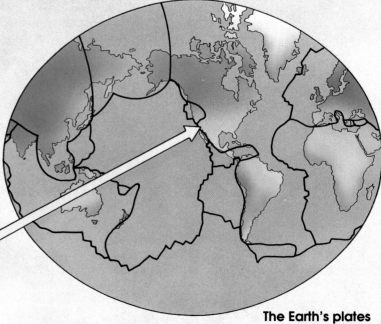

The Earth's plates

EARTHQUAKES

Earthquakes occur when two plates suddenly move toward or away from each other. There are about half a million earthquakes a year, mostly occurring under the sea. Earthquakes on land can cause a lot of damage. Huge cracks can open up and rock slides plunge down.

The Richter scale measures earthquake power, starting at 1. Each whole number higher means the quake is ten times stronger than one rated a whole number below. An earthquake rated 7 is as strong as a nuclear bomb.

VOLCANOES

Volcanoes occur when hot, liquid rock called lava seeps up from the Earth's mantle layer through cracks in the crust. Sometimes it oozes out quietly. But if gases have built up underground, the pressure causes a huge explosion. Lava, rocks, and ash shoot upward and when they cool and harden, they form a cone or crater around the hole they have made.

There are over 800 active volcanoes situated along the Earth's fault lines. They lie under water as well as on land, and about 50 to 60 erupt every year.

Hundreds of years may pass between eruptions. During that time volcanoes are termed dormant. When a volcano no longer erupts at all, it is called extinct.

A volcanic island forming

Volcanic eruptions have formed thousands of ocean islands. One example is the island of Surtsey near Iceland. In 1963, the sea started to boil and soon the top of a volcano appeared above the waves. Three weeks later, the island had grown to its present size. Its name, Surtsey, is from the Icelandic god of fire.

ROCKS AND FOSSILS

Rocks originate in the mantle layer beneath the Earth's crust as hot, liquid lava called magma. This material bubbles up to the surface during volcanic eruptions, then it cools and hardens. The three different types of rock are igneous, sedimentary, and metamorphic.

Granite rock face

When liquid magma seeps out onto the Earth's surface and cools down, it becomes igneous rock and is very hard. An example of a hard igneous type of rock is granite.

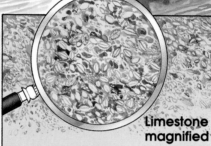

Limestone magnified

Sedimentary rocks consist of compacted layers of sand, rock pieces, shells, and the remains of tiny sea animals. One example of a sedimentary rock is limestone.

Marble

Sometimes igneous or sedimentary rocks plunge back into the mantle, where they change into metamorphic rock. For instance, limestone can change into marble.

FOSSILS

A fossil is the shape or imprint of an animal or plant found in rock.

A fossil forms when the soft parts of a dead animal or plant rot and mud or clay covers the hard parts. When the mud eventually hardens into rock, it preserves the shape of the dead body as a fossil.

Fossils are found only in sedimentary rock.

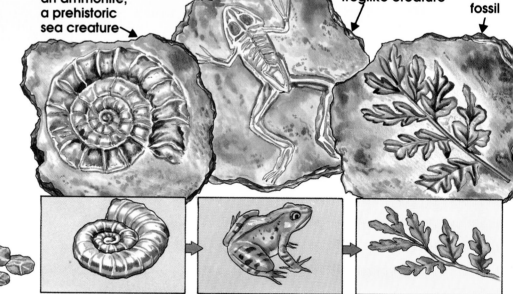

The fossil of an ammonite, a prehistoric sea creature

The fossil of a froglike creature

A leaf fossil

GEMS

Gems grow as crystals in rock. They vary in shape, color, and hardness. Diamonds are the hardest natural material. Gem fields lie in South Africa, India, Sri Lanka, Myanmar, and South America.

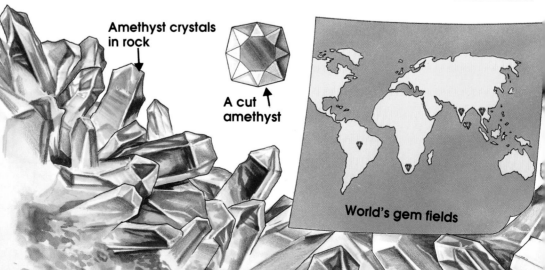

Amethyst crystals in rock

A cut amethyst

World's gem fields

SHAPING THE EARTH

When crustal plates collide, mountains may form as layers of rock squeeze together and thrust upward into huge folds.

The Himalayas and the European Alps are fold mountains formed between 20 and 70 million years ago. The oldest mountains, in Norway, Scotland, and Wales, date back some 400 million years.

Fold mountains caused by plate collision

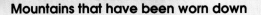

Mountains that have been worn down

Mountains gradually wear down from ice, wind, and water. About 3.5 inches (9 cm) may wear away in 1,000 years.

As mountains wear down, their shapes change from angular to more rounded.

HOW VALLEYS FORM

As a river flows downhill, it picks up pieces of loose rock that grind against the river-bank, wearing it away and carving out a V-shaped valley.

The Grand Canyon is the largest and deepest gorge, or valley, in the world. The Colorado River carved it, flowing at 30 mph (48 kph), carrying small rocks and stones. The canyon is over 5,000 feet (1,500 m) deep and 13 miles (21 km) wide in some places. It widens and deepens each year.

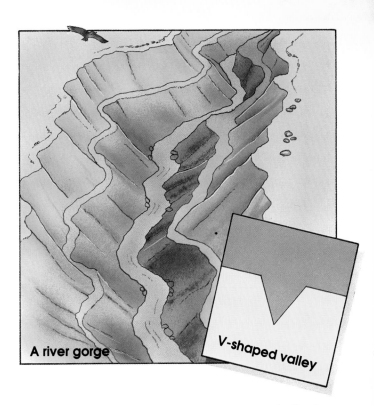

A river gorge

V-shaped valley

U-shaped valley

A glacier

Some valleys result from the action of glaciers, or large slow-moving rivers of ice (see page 22).

Glaciers occur when snow from high up in a mountain range turns to ice and flows smoothly downhill, often following a valley shape left by a river.

As it travels along, a glacier picks up debris, such as rocks and stones. These gradually grind down the valley floor, changing its shape from a V to a U.

DAY AND NIGHT

The Earth takes one year to orbit the Sun. As it travels, it spins, making one complete turn every 24 hours.

For 12 hours, half the Earth faces the Sun and has daytime, while the other half of the Earth faces away from the Sun and has nighttime. Then, for the next 12 hours, the sunny side faces away, and day and night are reversed.

During the day, the Sun looks as though it moves across the sky. But this effect is from the Earth spinning, and in reality the Sun does not move around the Earth at all.

THE SEASONS

The Earth tilts to one side as it travels around the Sun. This means that for a few months of each year half of the Earth tilts toward the Sun and gets the hottest rays, while the other half tilts away and gets cooler rays. This position gradually reverses through the year.

This tilt causes the seasons. When it is Summer in the northern half, or Northern Hemisphere, of the Earth, it is Winter in the other half, or Southern Hemisphere. Later, Winter and Summer change places. In Fall and Spring, the two hemispheres are an equal distance from the Sun's rays.

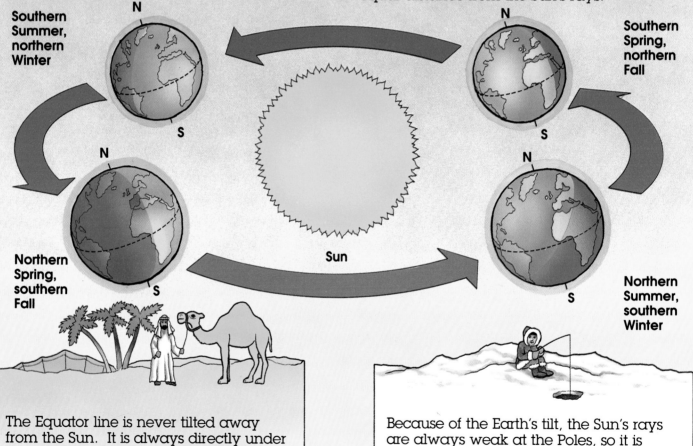

Southern Summer, northern Winter

Southern Spring, northern Fall

Northern Spring, southern Fall

Sun

Northern Summer, southern Winter

The Equator line is never tilted away from the Sun. It is always directly under its strongest rays. The areas on either side of the line, called the Tropics, always have hot weather.

Because of the Earth's tilt, the Sun's rays are always weak at the Poles, so it is always cold and icy there. In Winter it is dark nearly all the time, and in Summer there is 24-hour daylight.

EARTH FACT FINDER

The world's highest mountain is Mount Everest in Nepal and Tibet in the Himalayan mountain range. It is over 29,000 feet (8,800 m) in height.

The longest mountain range, the undersea Indian/East Pacific Cordillera, runs 19,200 miles (30,900 km) from the Gulf of Aden in the Middle East to the Gulf of California, Mexico.

Quito, Ecuador, reputedly has the world's ideal climate. It is always warm and sunny there. The temperature at night rarely drops below 46°F (7.8°C) and may reach 72°F (22°C) during the day. There are occasional rain showers but never enough to soak the inhabitants.

The largest desert on Earth is the Sahara in North Africa. It covers an area of over 3 million square miles (7.8 million sq km), almost one-third of Africa.

The highest sand dunes in the world are in the Algerian region of the Sahara Desert. Some measure up to 1,410 feet (430 m) high, nearly as high as the tallest building in the world!

The world's highest active volcano is Ojos del Salado in Argentina. It is over 22,500 feet (6,900 m) high.

Mauna Loa, Hawaii, is the world's largest active volcano. It has a dome 75 miles (120 km) long and 64 miles (100 km) wide, and its name means "long mountain." It erupts on average once every 3.5 years.

One of the worst earthquakes in world history happened in Lisbon, Portugal, in 1755. It destroyed this major city in just six minutes.

The shock of the quake traveled for thousands of miles, and a giant wave 56 feet (17 m) high, generated by the Earth's movement, drowned hundreds of people.

The lowest place on land is the Dead Sea in Israel and Jordan, the saltiest lake in the world. Its surface is nearly 1,300 feet (400 m) below sea level.

The deepest cave is found in France. It is called the Réseau Jean Bernard, and is over 5,000 feet (1,500 m) below the surface.

The longest lava flow from a volcanic eruption occurred in Iceland in 1783. The lava from a volcano called Laki flowed a distance of over 40 miles (64 km). The thickness of lava flows can vary up to 65 feet (20 m).

WEATHER

The Earth shelters beneath a layer of air called the atmosphere. The constantly moving air causes the world's weather to change.

The atmosphere reaches far above the ground, but weather changes occur only in the bottom six miles (10 km). Airplanes usually fly above this level to avoid strong winds and storms.

WHY IT RAINS

Rain falls to Earth and then returns to the sky as invisible mist called water vapor, or moisture. You can see the process below.

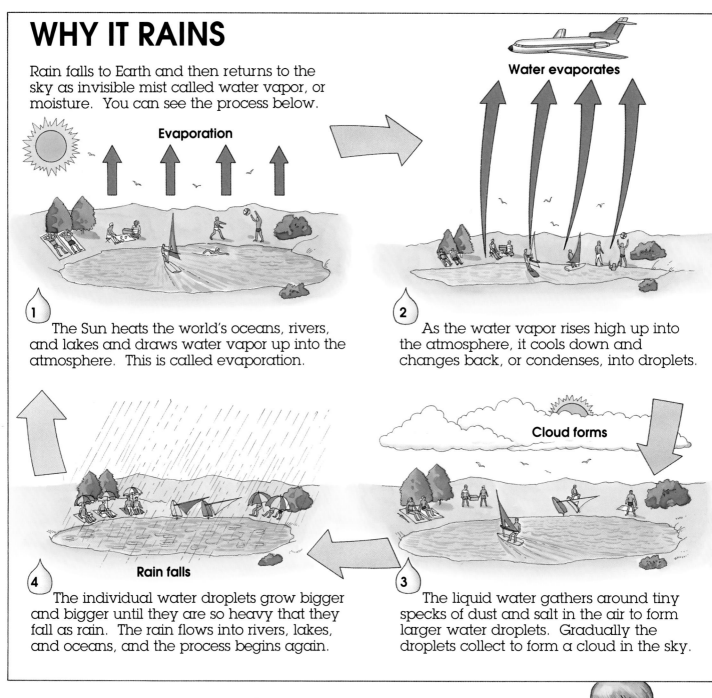

Evaporation

Water evaporates

1 The Sun heats the world's oceans, rivers, and lakes and draws water vapor up into the atmosphere. This is called evaporation.

2 As the water vapor rises high up into the atmosphere, it cools down and changes back, or condenses, into droplets.

Cloud forms

Rain falls

4 The individual water droplets grow bigger and bigger until they are so heavy that they fall as rain. The rain flows into rivers, lakes, and oceans, and the process begins again.

3 The liquid water gathers around tiny specks of dust and salt in the air to form larger water droplets. Gradually the droplets collect to form a cloud in the sky.

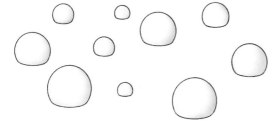

Raindrops are not really tear-shaped, as most people think. They are round with a flattened base, as shown above.

Water vapor rises

Dish empty

You can see how water evaporates if you put a dish of water outside on a hot, sunny day. After a while the water will disappear.

THE WIND

Wind is moving air. The air around the Earth moves because it is heated by the Sun. The warm air rises upward and cold air flows into the space left beneath.

You can see how hot air rises by watching a hot-air balloon. To go higher, the balloonist turns up a gas flame to make the air inside the balloon warm. To go lower, the balloonist turns down the flame so that the air in the balloon will cool down.

Some winds flow in regular patterns around the Earth, as shown on the right. They result as hot air rises up from the tropical regions and cold air flows from the Earth's Poles into its place.

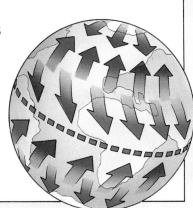

SNOW, HAIL, AND FOG

When a cloud is very cold, its water droplets freeze into ice crystals and fall to Earth as snow. At the polar ice caps, it is so cold that water *always* falls to the ground as snow. Deep beneath the top layer lies snow that fell thousands of years ago. It has never been warm enough for it to melt.

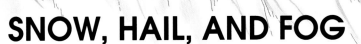

As ice crystals fall, they collide with each other to make patterned snowflake shapes.
No two snowflake shapes are ever alike.

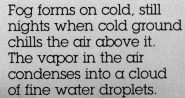

Hailstones begin as tiny ice pellets in high clouds. They gradually grow bigger as water freezes onto them. A hailstone consists of lots of frozen layers, like an onion's.

Fog forms on cold, still nights when cold ground chills the air above it. The vapor in the air condenses into a cloud of fine water droplets.

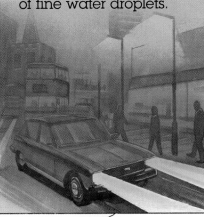

13

CLOUD SHAPES

Ten different types of clouds exist. Each one has a different shape that gives clues to the coming weather.

Stratocumulus clouds layer across the sky. In winter, they can indicate snow.

▲ Cumulus clouds are fluffy and white. Small ones signal fine weather to come.

▲ Cirrus clouds look like long wisps, often with flicked-back tails. They signal rain.

▲ Cirrocumulus clouds look like ripples across the sky. They promise cold weather.

▲ Cirrostratus clouds make a thin veil across the sky. They warn of rain or snow.

▲ Altocumulus clouds make streaks and patches. They herald weather changes.

▲ Nimbostratus clouds are dark and low, covering the Sun. *Nimbo* is Latin for rain.

▲ Cumulonimbus clouds are billowing storm clouds that tower into the sky.

▲ Stratus clouds foreshadow rain or snow. They spread out in a low gray layer.

▲ Altostratus clouds make patchy gray layers across the sky, telling of rain.

RAINBOW MAKING

Rainbows appear when the Sun comes out on a rainy day. To see one, you need to stand with the Sun behind you so that it shines on the raindrops and they reflect the light back toward you. Normally, the Sun's light looks clear, but it is actually made up of different colors. When sunlight passes through raindrops, it bends and splits up into separate bands of colors.

STORMS

Around 2,000 thunderstorms take place in the world at any one time. They occur when the air is hot and humid. This rises and forms cumulonimbus thunder clouds in the sky.

Electricity builds up in a thunder cloud and discharges as lightning. A lightning flash heats up the air in its path, and the air expands quickly, making a booming thunder noise. Thunder and lightning occur together, but we see the lightning first because light travels faster than sound.

Storm

Tornado

KILLER STORMS

Hurricanes are powerful swirling masses of cloud, wind, and rain. They begin over warm, tropical oceans and move westward, dying out as they reach land.

Tornadoes occur mostly in the mid-western US. These funnel-shaped storms result from hot air spinning as it rises.

DROUGHTS AND MONSOONS

Monsoons are seasonal winds that bring torrential rain to the Tropics, the area around the Equator. The monsoon season lasts a couple of months or so, depending on the area. Sometimes too much rain brings flooding. At other times, the rains fail, causing drought.

Monsoon rain

In a drought period, plants and crops can die off through lack of rain, causing great hardship and starvation to local people.

Rain can fall after cloud seeding. Planes spray chemical crystals into a cloud, and water vapor condenses on the crystals to form raindrops. But this can only happen if there is a cloud in the first place!

15

WEATHER FORECASTS

Scientists who study the weather are called meteorologists. They use all kinds of measurements, such as temperatures and wind speeds, to help them predict weather changes. They get help from weather satellites that beam down pictures of the weather seen from far above the Earth. Storms or fine weather patterns show up on the pictures.

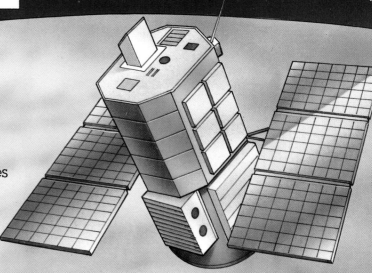

Weather satellite

SPECIAL WEATHER

Large cities can make their own clouds. The buildings warm the air around them and the warm air rises and forms a hazy cloud.

When air meets a mountain, the air must rise. As it gets higher, it cools and forms a cloud. It often rains and snows near mountain areas.

Coastlines are often windy because the Sun heats land more quickly than water. Warm land air rises and cool sea air flows in underneath.

WEATHER CHANGES

Sometimes the weather changes accidentally through human-caused pollution. Above some large cities, chimney smoke mixes with fog to form smog that is dirty and dangerous to breathe.

Harmful chemicals from factories and cars can mix with water vapor in the air to produce acid rain that kills plants and gradually eats into metal and buildings.

WEATHER FACT FINDER

The sky is blue because sunlight consists of several different color bands (see page 14). When the Sun's light reaches the Earth's atmosphere, the blue color band spreads out in all directions. All the other color bands pass through the atmosphere down to the Earth. Cloudy weather blocks the blue color from view.

Kauai, Hawaii, has the largest number of rainy days per year. It rains up to 350 days annually there.
The driest place on Earth is the Chilean Atacama Desert, where it seldom rains.
The windiest place is Commonwealth Bay, Antarctica, where winds sometimes measure up to 200 mph (320 kph).

The air in the atmosphere presses down on the Earth. For example, if you stand at sea level, the weight of the atmospheric air on you equals the weight of a family car.
However, you don't feel this because your body has its own inside pressure pushing outward. The two forces balance each other so that you remain comfortable and cannot feel any pressure.

Dallol, Ethiopia, is the hottest place on Earth. Temperatures there can average up to 94°F (34°C) a year.
The coldest place on Earth is in Antarctica, where the average yearly temperature can be as low as -72°F (-58°C). Human skin would freeze in seconds if exposed in these conditions.
The sunniest place on Earth is the Sahara Desert, where the Sun shines for more hours per year than anywhere.

The biggest hailstones ever reported killed 92 people in Bangladesh in 1986. Some weighed up to 2.25 pounds (1 kg). Sometimes tornadoes pick up objects that later fall to Earth. For example, in 1973, in the French village of Brignoles, there was a freak storm when thousands of toads fell out of the sky! A tornado had passed over their breeding ground and picked them up.

Two million years ago the Earth was in the grip of an Ice Age. Since then the climate has gradually warmed up. Some scientists think that our weather is very gradually getting colder again. But others think that the temperature is getting progressively warmer due to pollution in the air. This creates a thick layer that prevents heat from escaping the atmosphere. It is sometimes called the greenhouse effect.

A network of satellites provides a weather watch for the whole world. The satellites record the weather picture over different areas of the planet below them.
The satellites don't take real photographs. Instead they convert what they see into a stream of signals that can be interpreted by a computer and formed into a picture showing things like cloud cover. You can often see these satellite pictures on TV weather forecasts.

SEAS AND RIVERS

About 70% of the Earth's surface lies beneath water. Most of this is salt water and forms the oceans — the Pacific, Atlantic, Indian, Arctic, and Antarctic.

Just over 2% of the Earth's water is in the form of ice in the Arctic and Antarctic regions. The rest makes up the world's rivers, lakes, and underground springs.

THE OCEANS

The Pacific Ocean is the largest and deepest ocean, covering nearly a third of the Earth's surface. It measures up to 11,000 miles (17,600 km) across. Next in size is the Atlantic, then the Indian, the Antarctic, and the Arctic, which is the smallest and shallowest ocean.

Each ocean is divided into smaller areas called seas.

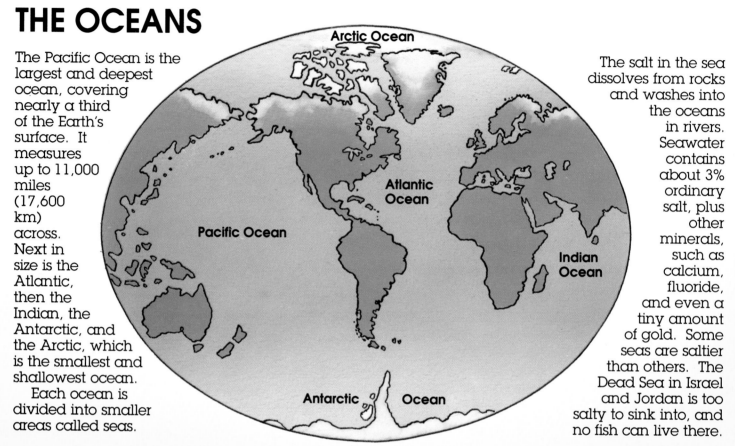

The salt in the sea dissolves from rocks and washes into the oceans in rivers. Seawater contains about 3% ordinary salt, plus other minerals, such as calcium, fluoride, and even a tiny amount of gold. Some seas are saltier than others. The Dead Sea in Israel and Jordan is too salty to sink into, and no fish can live there.

TIDES

Tides result from the gravity forces of the Moon and Sun pulling on the Earth as it spins, causing sea levels to rise and fall.

When the Sun, Moon, and Earth are in line, as during a new or full Moon, the forces combine and cause very high tides called spring tides. When the Sun and Moon are at right angles with the Earth, as during a half Moon, the Sun's force counteracts the Moon's force, resulting in the very low neap tides.

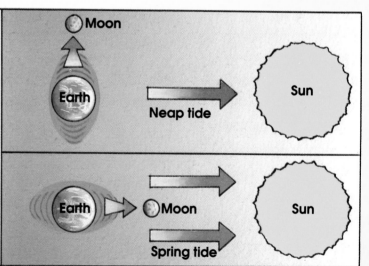

WAVES

Ocean waves result from the wind blowing on the sea and rippling the water. Stronger winds make larger waves.

EROSION

Waves can change the shape of a coastline by eroding it, pounding away and breaking off pieces of rock. Seashore pebbles are rocks broken up by waves and ground against each other until they become smooth. Soft rock eventually wears to mud. Harder rock grinds into sand.

Waves can wear away a cliff base until the top eventually falls.

If there is a crack in a cliff, the sea will hollow it into a cave.

If waves pound a headland from both sides, an archway can form.

THE SEABED

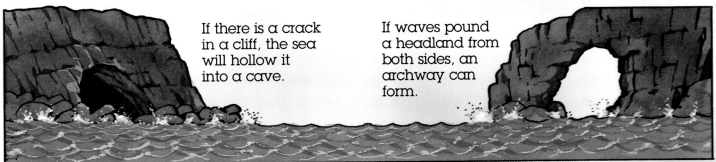

The oceans flow around the world's continents. Around each continent lies an area of shallow seabed called a continental shelf.

At the edge of a continental shelf the seabed slopes steeply down to an area called the abyssal plain, where there may be high underwater mountain ranges and deep trenches.

Continental shelf

Abyssal plain

CURRENTS

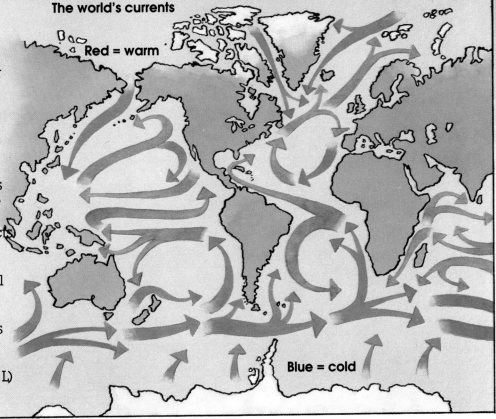

Ocean water sweeps around the world in regular paths called currents that develop from wind and warm water moving away from the Equator and cold water flowing in to take its place.

Currents absorb the Sun's heat. Depending on where the currents are, they can be cold or warm. This affects the climate on any nearby land. For example, wind blowing off a warm sea will bring a mild climate.

The West Wind Drift, the world's largest current, flows around the globe, north of Antarctica. It moves over 70 billion gallons (270 billion L) of water a second!

The world's currents

Red = warm

Blue = cold

RIVERS

A river starts life at its source, often a spring high up in a mountain range. When rain falls, it swells the spring water so that a stream forms and flows downhill. Other streams, called tributaries, join it and help the stream grow. You can see the life of a river illustrated on the left.

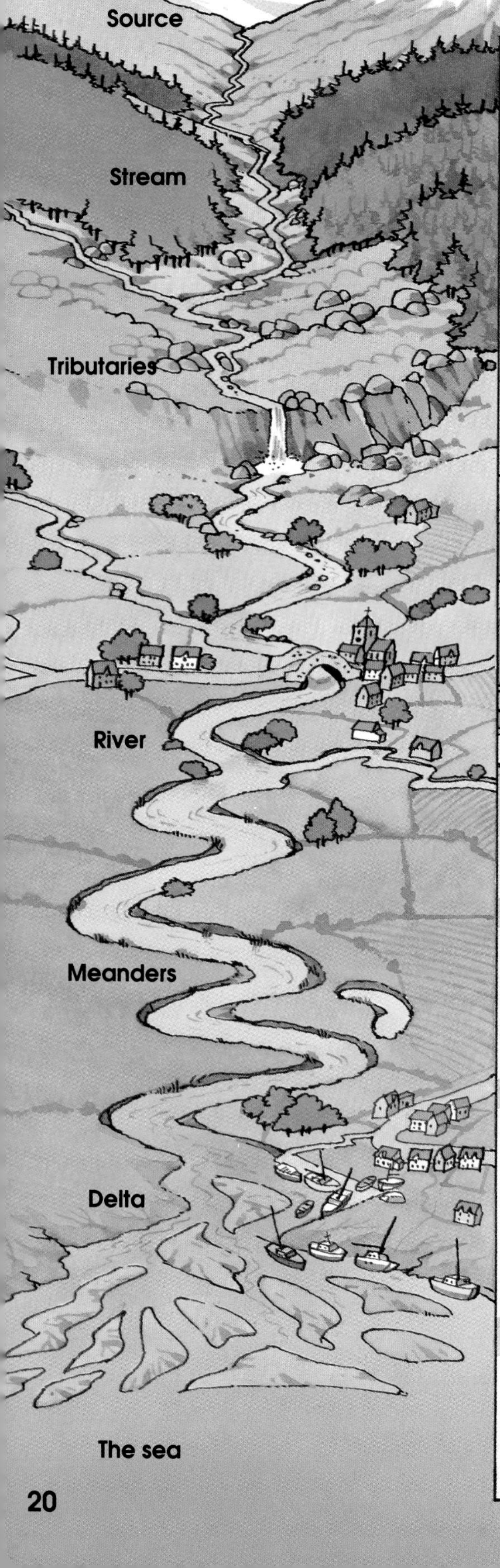

Source

Stream

Tributaries

River

Meanders

Delta

The sea

RIVER FEATURES

In its first, fast-flowing stage, the river wears away rocks and stones in its bed and carries them along, wearing them down to mud and sand. As the river reaches flatter ground, it slows down and drops some of its load in the riverbed or along its banks. The rest it carries toward its mouth.

The Mississippi River, the longest river in the United States, carries 500 million tons of mud and fine sand toward the sea every year. At its mouth it drops its load, forming large, sloping mounds. The river flows around these in many small branches. This is called a river delta.

Mackenzie Delta, Canada

When a river slows down, it loses the power to grind away hard rock. Instead, it loops around the rock, finding an easier route over softer sand or mud. The curve it makes is called a meander.

Sometimes a river will bend around so much that the loop it makes joins up at the base.

The river starts to flow across the short route at the base, leaving the loop to form a lake called an oxbow that gradually silts up.

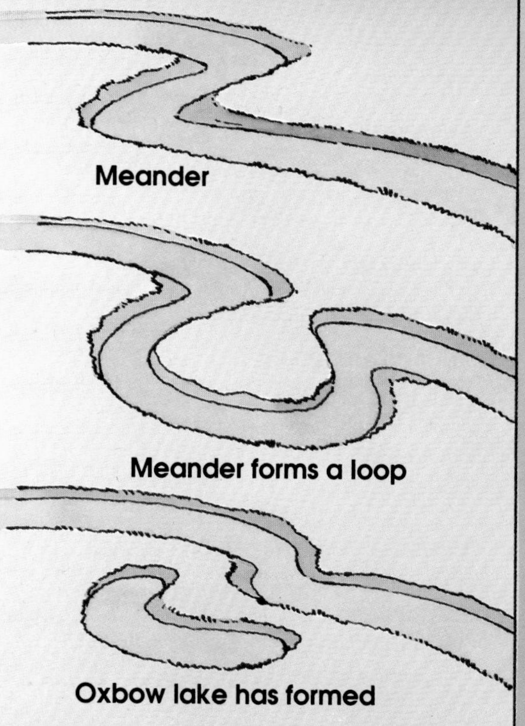

Meander

Meander forms a loop

Oxbow lake has formed

UNDERGROUND WATER

Falling rain can trickle through cracks in soft rocks, such as limestone, gradually wearing the cracks into underground tunnels. Eventually an underground river may develop and hollow out caves in the rock.

The biggest underground lake is reputedly the Lost Sea 300 feet (90 m) below ground in Tennessee, with an area of 4.5 acres (1.8 ha).

As water drips from a cave roof, mineral deposits build up to form stalactites. Stalagmites form where the water drips on the ground.

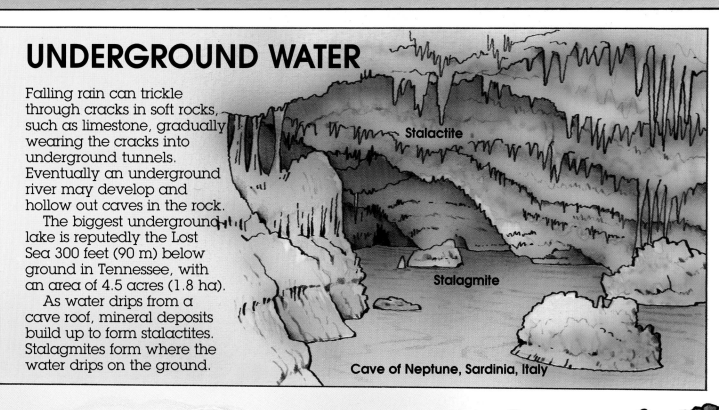

Stalactite

Stalagmite

Cave of Neptune, Sardinia, Italy

GEYSERS

Geysers, or hot springs, form when underground water heats up from volcanic activity. It bubbles to the surface through cracks, or gushes upward in jets of scalding water and steam.

One of the best-known geysers is Old Faithful in Yellowstone National Park. It erupts from the ground about once every hour.

WATERFALLS

Waterfalls occur where a hard band of rock crosses a riverbed. The water can't wear it down easily, so it runs over it to a lower level.

The highest waterfall in the world is Angel Falls, Venezuela. It is over 3,200 feet (970 m) high.

Water gradually wears away the edge of a waterfall. In the last 10,000 years, Niagara Falls wore back seven miles (11 km).

Angel Falls

ICE AND GLACIERS

The Arctic

North Pole
+

Greenland

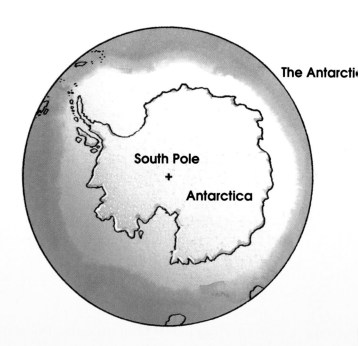

The Antarctic

South Pole
+

Antarctica

The ice sheets at the Poles hold about 2% of the Earth's water. If they ever melted, the world's sea level would rise by about 200 feet (60 m)! The largest ice sheets lie in Greenland and Antarctica.

The ice sheets are the remains of the last Ice Age 12,000 years ago, when a third of the Earth's surface was covered by ice 650 feet (195 m) thick. Today's Antarctic ice sheet is 2.5 miles (4 km) thick in parts.

Huge pieces of ice called icebergs often break off ice sheets and drift, sometimes over long distances.

A collision with a large iceberg could easily sink a ship. Only about 1/7th of the full size may show above the surface of the water.

Icebergs can be quite noisy, creaking as they move. Some of them are so loud that they are called growlers.

Floating iceberg

Glacier river

About 10% of the Earth's surface lies under glaciers, rivers of ice forming high up in snowy mountain ranges (see p. 9). As layer upon layer of snow builds up, the bottom layers harden into ice and start to move downhill. Glaciers can move up to 200 feet (60 m) a day, but most move only an inch or two. Earthen debris that a glacier piles up is called a moraine.

SEAS AND RIVERS FACT FINDER

The shortest river in the world is the Roe River in Montana. It is only 200 feet (61 m) long from its source to the Missouri River.

The largest river basin is the land drained by the Amazon. It covers nearly three million square miles (7.8 million sq km) of South American jungle.

The deepest part of the oceans, also the deepest point on Earth, is the Marianas Trench in the Pacific Ocean. It measures 35,840 feet (10,900 m) deep.

In 1960 divers explored the trench in a bathyscaphe, a small reinforced submarine. They reached a depth of 35,820 feet (10,900 m) where they found flatfish similar to sole.

The world's largest lake is an inland sea, due to its salt water. The Caspian Sea in the USSR and Iran is 760 miles (1,220 km) long and covers nearly 140,000 square miles (362,600 sq km).

The largest freshwater lake is Lake Superior. It lies in the United States and Canada. This huge lake covers 31,800 square miles (82,360 sq km).

The greatest difference in tides is found in the Bay of Fundy, Canada. The biggest difference between high and low tide is nearly 55 feet (16.8 m).

The highest wave ever observed was estimated as 112 feet (34 m) high! Seen from a passing ship, it occurred during a Pacific Ocean hurricane in 1933.

The largest bay in the world is Hudson Bay in northern Canada. It has a shoreline that stretches over 7,600 miles (12,200 km).

In 1610, the English explorer Henry Hudson sailed into the bay, thinking he had found a sea route from Europe through to China. But his crew mutinied and cast him adrift, never to be seen again.

The longest rivers in the world are the Amazon in South America and the Nile in Egypt.

The Amazon is nearly 4,200 miles (6,800 km) long from its source in the Andes to its mouth in the South Atlantic. The Nile is 4,145 miles (6,700 km) long from Burundi in Africa to the Mediterranean Sea.

The longest known glacier is the Lambert Glacier in the Antarctic. It is 250 miles (400 km) long and up to 40 miles (64 km) wide.

The largest ever iceberg measured an enormous 12,000 square miles (31,100 sq km)! It was floating off the coast of Antarctica.

The tallest iceberg ever, one near Greenland, was 550 feet (168 m) tall.

PLANTS

Plants first appeared on Earth hundreds of millions of years ago. Today there are over 400,000 recorded species. They are vital to us because they produce the oxygen that all animals need in order to survive. We also use them for many practical purposes, such as food, clothing material, medicines, and dyes.

PLANT COLOR AND FOOD

Green plants make their own food by a process called photosynthesis. To help them do this, they contain a substance called chlorophyll that is a bright green color.

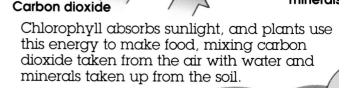

Sunlight

Carbon dioxide

Water and minerals

Chlorophyll absorbs sunlight, and plants use this energy to make food, mixing carbon dioxide taken from the air with water and minerals taken up from the soil.

OXYGEN AND ENERGY

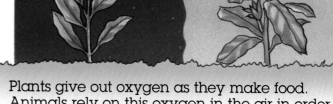

During the day, when there is plenty of sunlight, plants photosynthesize. At night, when there is no light, they stop making food.

The plants convert the food they make into energy to help them grow, and they continue to do this even when it's dark.

Plants give out oxygen as they make food. Animals rely on this oxygen in the air in order to breathe.

Animals give out carbon dioxide as they breathe, and plants use this when they photosynthesize.

Stomata

PLANTS AND WATER

A plant takes up water from the soil through its roots. It rises up through tubes inside the stem, keeping the plant firm and upright. A thirsty plant will soon start to droop.

When it reaches the leaves, some of the water is used up to make food. The rest is released as water vapor through tiny holes, called stomata, in the underside of the leaf. This process of losing water is called transpiration.

FLOWERS

Most plants have flowers. These contain the male and female parts needed to make seeds that eventually grow into new plants. Some species, such as poppies, bear both male and female parts on the same flower, as shown below. Some other types of plant bear separate male and female flowers.

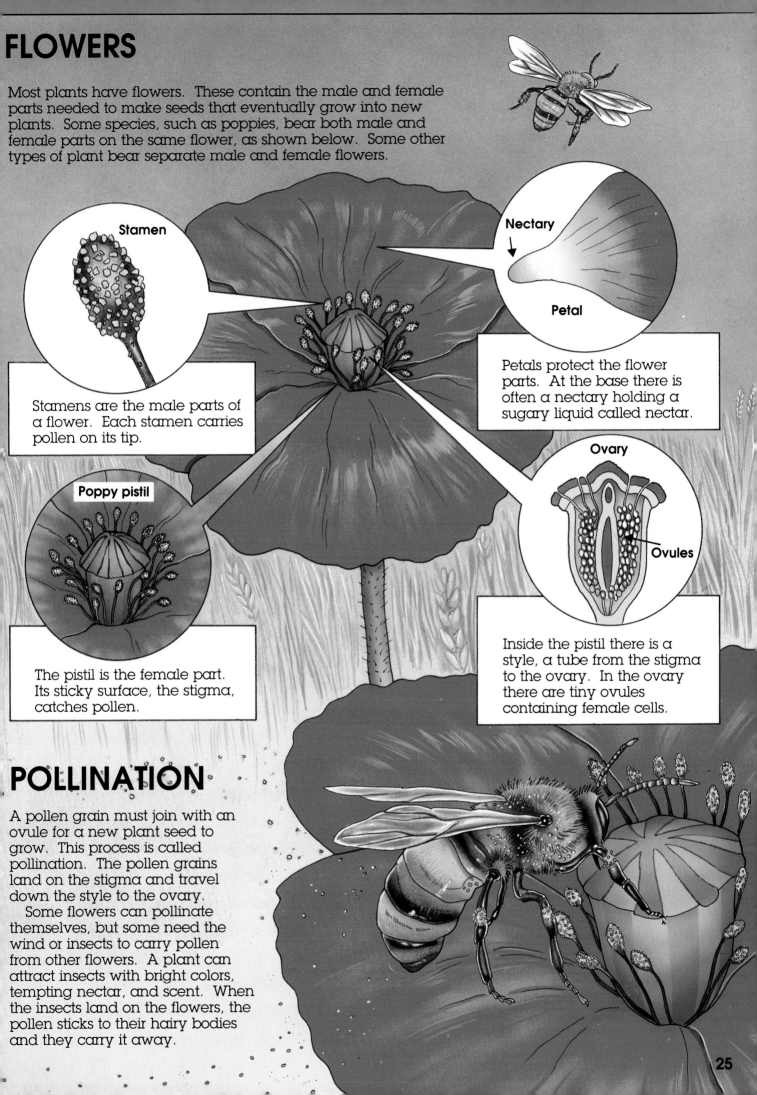

Stamen

Stamens are the male parts of a flower. Each stamen carries pollen on its tip.

Nectary

Petal

Petals protect the flower parts. At the base there is often a nectary holding a sugary liquid called nectar.

Poppy pistil

The pistil is the female part. Its sticky surface, the stigma, catches pollen.

Ovary

Ovules

Inside the pistil there is a style, a tube from the stigma to the ovary. In the ovary there are tiny ovules containing female cells.

POLLINATION

A pollen grain must join with an ovule for a new plant seed to grow. This process is called pollination. The pollen grains land on the stigma and travel down the style to the ovary.

Some flowers can pollinate themselves, but some need the wind or insects to carry pollen from other flowers. A plant can attract insects with bright colors, tempting nectar, and scent. When the insects land on the flowers, the pollen sticks to their hairy bodies and they carry it away.

TREES

Trees are green plants that have a woody stem or trunk. The first trees appeared on Earth about 330 million years ago. From fossil evidence, scientists think that they we similar to the pines and spruces of today.

TREE GROUPS

Trees such as pine and spruce are called conifers. Trees such as oak and fruit trees are called broad-leaved.

You can identify a tree by the shape of its leaves and from its fruit and seeds. The tree's overall shape will also help you decide which group it belongs to.

Oak leaf and acorn

Horse chestnut leaf with chestnut

Scotch pine cone

Norway spruce cone

Douglas fir cone

Broad-leaved trees have either simple or compound leaves. Simple leaves, such as oak, have one single blade. Compound leaves, such as horse chestnut leaves, consist of several small leaves growing on one stalk.

Broad-leaved trees are bush-shaped. They grow all kinds of fruit, such as nuts, apples, cherries, and pears.

Conifer leaves are called needles. They are covered with a waxy coating to protect them from winter cold.

Conifers produce their seeds in cones of different shapes and sizes, and the trees themselves are cone-shaped.

EVERGREEN AND DECIDUOUS

Evergreen tree

Deciduous tree

Deciduous leaf in Fall

Most broad-leaved trees lose their leaves for Winter because there is not enough sunlight for the leaves to make food. Most conifers keep their leaves all year round.

The trees that shed their leaves are called deciduous. The ones that keep their leaves are called evergreen.

Evergreen trees tend to grow in cool temperatures. In the Northern Hemisphere there are many extensive conifer forests.

Deciduous trees tend to grow where summers are warm and winters are cool.

In the Fall, the leaves on these trees start to change color from green to red, orange, or yellow. This is because the green chlorophyll coloring in the leaf breaks down through lack of sunlight, allowing other colors to show up.

Eventually the leaves die through lack of food and fall off the tree. New leaves appear in Spring, when the sunlight increases.

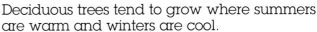

TREE RINGS

The wood in the middle of a tree trunk is called heartwood. Around it lies a layer of sapwood that carries minerals up through the tree and that also contains stores of food.

Each year, a tree grows a new ring of wood around its trunk. A wide tree ring shows that the year was good for growing. A narrow ring shows that it was probably a dry year, one poor for growth.

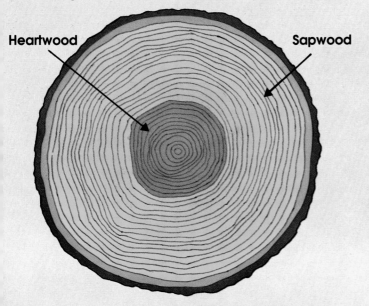

Heartwood

Sapwood

BARK

A tree is covered with a tough layer of wood called bark. It protects the tree from harmful plants, animals, and weather.

Bark is dead wood. It cannot stretch as the trunk grows, so it splits, peels off, and is replaced with a new layer.

Tree bark develops a particular pattern and coloring depending on its species. Some different types are shown below.

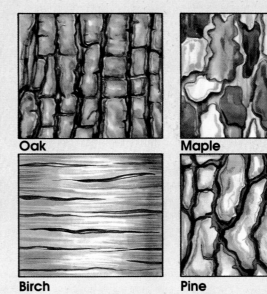

Oak

Maple

Birch

Pine

27

FRUITS AND SEEDS

Pea pod

After pollination, plant seeds begin to develop. They are protected inside fruits. For example, a pea pod is a fruit and the peas inside are seeds.

Pods, berries, and nuts are all fruits with seeds inside.
   Seeds such as apple pips and cherry stones are surrounded by very thick fleshy fruit.

Eventually a seed must leave its fruit so that it can become a new plant. Insects and birds help to carry away seeds, often by eating them.

TRAVELING SEEDS

Some plants have unusual ways of spreading seeds.

Puffball

The giant puffball is a type of fungus that can grow up to 11.5 inches (30 cm) across.
   Each puffball makes about seven million seeds, called spores, that the fungus shoots high into the air to be carried away by the wind.

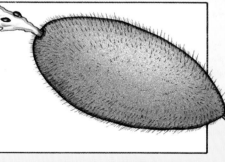

The fruit of the squirting cucumber bursts open when it is ripe, shooting seeds out at up to 62 mph (100 kph). They can travel 26 feet (8 m) away from the original plant.

Pine cones are a type of fruit containing seeds pollinated by the wind.
   After pollination, the cone's scales harden and close up. When the seeds are ripe, the cones open to expose them.
   The sycamore fruit has two wings with a seed in between. When the fruit falls, it catches the breeze and spins away from the parent tree.

Sycamore wing

Oak seedling

Oak tree

Seeds will only grow into plants when the soil and weather are good. For example, only about one in a million acorns lands in the right place to grow into an oak tree.

UNUSUAL PLANTS

Flies are attracted to the Venus' Flytrap by the colorful insides of its leaves. But the leaves are hinged traps that snap shut when insects land on them.

It takes the leaves about half an hour to squash a fly and up to 14 days to absorb it. Then the trap opens again.

Pitcher plants ▶ have an ingenious way of catching insects for food.
Each leaf is shaped like a jug, or pitcher, with a deep hollow and a lid on top to keep out rain. Insects land on the rim of the leaf in search of nectar, but they fall down the slippery sides of the pitcher and drown in the liquid inside.

▲ Lichens are tiny plant pairs of algae and fungi that grow on rocks in patches of green, white, brown, or yellow. They eat rock by making acids that crumble it. Their roots then absorb minerals from the pieces. In this way, they slowly break the rock down into soil.

◀ Stone plants have leaves disguised as pebbles, so that they are well hidden from hungry animals. They show up clearly only when their flowers bloom between the leaves.

◀ *Welwitschia mirabilis* grows in the Namibian Desert in Africa. It can live for over a hundred years, but it grows only two leaves that both split into long, thin strips. The plant takes about 20 years to grow its first flower.

◀ Lianas are climbing plants found in tropical rain forests. They cling to other plants, using these as a support to reach up to the sunlight. Liana stems hang down to the ground like ropes and can be up to 1,000 feet (300 m) long. Animals use them to swing from tree to tree.

USEFUL PLANTS

Paddy field

Rubber trees

All living things depend on plants because these come first in nature's food chain. Plants provide the food for small animals that in turn are eaten by larger animals.

Rice is the most widespread food plant that humans eat. People grow it in hot Asian regions. Because it needs plenty of water, they sow it in flooded areas called paddy fields.

Rubber, from the sap of the rubber tree, makes such products as tires. The rubber gatherer makes deep cuts in the bark and collects the sap, or latex, that runs out.

Rubber trees once grew only in the Amazon rain forests. In the 19th century, smuggled seeds grew into plants in London. They later went to Sri Lanka, Singapore, and Malaysia to start rubber plantations.

COAL AND OIL

Oil platform

Coal and oil are called fossil fuels because they formed millions of years ago from huge forests of moss and giant ferns. As they died, the plants fossilized and eventually turned to coal.

Oil formed from tiny plants and sea animals that died millions of years ago. They sank to the seabed to be covered by mud, eventually forming a black liquid. Oil often lies beneath the seabed.

Most of the paper we use comes from coniferous trees that are used because they grow quickly. The chopped wood soaks in water until it turns into soft pulp. After drying and pressing, the pulp becomes paper.

MEDICINES

Many of our medicines come from plants. For instance, quinine, used to treat malaria, comes from the bark of the tropical cinchona tree. Penicillin is a strong bacteria-killer extracted from a mold.

Herbs for centuries have helped cure illness. Many contain substances that have a marked effect on the human body.

MATERIALS

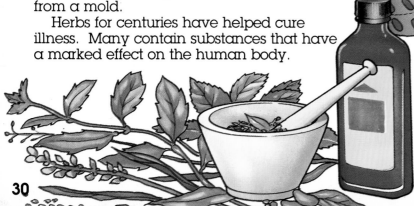
Cotton plant

The seeds of the cotton plant are covered in fluffy white fibers that people use to make thread for weaving into cotton cloth.

Linen is another example of cloth made from a plant. People weave it from the stem fibers of the flax plant. Flaxseeds, when ground up, produce linseed oil, useful for paint and other products.

PLANTS FACT FINDER

The largest flower is that of the stinking corpse lily found in the jungles of Asia. The plant is parasitic, that is, it lives off other plants as it winds around jungle tree vines. The flower can weigh up to 15 pounds (7 kg) and can grow up to 36 inches (90 cm) wide. It has a terrible rotting meat smell to attract insects such as flies.

The fastest-growing tree in the world is a Malaysian tree, *Albizzia falcata*, that grows up to 35 feet (10.5 m) in just one year.
The slowest-growing tree is the Sitka spruce, found above the Arctic Circle. It takes 98 years to grow 11 inches (28 cm).

The world's largest forested area stretches across Scandinavia and the northern USSR. It covers about 4.2 million square miles (11 million sq km), one-fourth of all the forest area in the world.
Increasing pollution destroys forests. Chemical waste from factory chimneys falls down in rain, killing them.

The biggest tree in the world is a giant sequoia, General Sherman, in Sequoia National Park, California. It is nearly 275 feet (84 m) tall and almost 115 feet (35 m) around.
The tallest tree in the world is a coast redwood, also in California. It stands nearly 368 feet (112 m) tall.

The oldest trees in the world are the bristlecone pines growing in Nevada and California. The oldest living specimen, named Methuselah, is about 4,600 years old.
The Chinese maiden-hair tree, or gingko, considered the oldest form of tree, first appeared about 160 million years ago.

The largest cacti are the saguaro cacti in the western US and Mexico. Saguaros grow only about one inch (2.5 cm) in the first year of their lives, but they can live to be about 200 years old. By this time they are 40-50 feet (12-15 m) tall and weigh around 10 tons. About nine tons is water stored in the leaves and stem.

A wild fig tree at the Echo Caves site in South Africa has the deepest measured plant roots in the world. They grow 400 feet (120 m) down into the ground. Experts can measure them because they can see them inside the caves.

The smallest trees grow close to the ground in places where they are protected from the cold and wind. Dwarf willows are one example. They may have branches 16 feet (5 m) long but they are often only about four inches (10 cm) tall.

Bamboo grows in India, the Far East, and China. It is one of the fastest-growing plants, and can sprout up to 36 inches (90 cm) in a day. Bamboo often reaches a total height of about 100 feet (30 m).

ANIMALS

About 70% of all the living species on Earth are animals, creatures that breathe in oxygen and must eat plants or other animals to survive.

There are over a million different kinds of animals, ranging from huge blue whales to tiny single-celled amoebas that can be seen only under a microscope.

ANIMAL GROUPS

When scientists classify animals, they divide them into different groups of related creatures. Below you can see some of the largest and most important groups.

The mammal group includes such varying creatures as bats, whales, platypuses, kangaroos, and humans.

There are over 700,000 known insect species. This group includes ants, butterflies, beetles, wasps, and lice.

The fish group includes such varying creatures as sharks, eels, and seahorses.

Most animals in the bird group can fly. But it also includes nonflying birds such as penguins.

The reptile group includes many different kinds of lizards, snakes, turtles, and crocodiles.

Amphibians can live on land and in water. Frogs, toads, and newts are examples.

The arachnid group of creatures includes spiders, scorpions, harvestmen, and mites.

There are many other smaller animal groups. See a few of the more common ones below.

The coelenterates include jellyfish, sea anemones, and coral that is made up from millions of tiny sea animals.

The tiny coral creatures form hard skeletons around their soft bodies. Eventually these build up into a reef.

Crustaceans include prawns, barnacles, and crabs, all with hard outer shells for protecting their soft bodies.

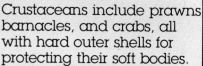
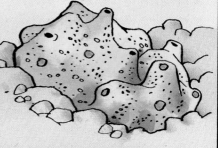

There are over 65,000 species of mollusks, including snails, slugs, clams, limpets, and octopuses.

The largest bivalve is the giant clam from Southeast Asia. Its shell can weigh over a quarter of a ton.

Sponges are in their own group, the poriferans. A natural bath sponge is the skeleton of the animal.

INSECTS

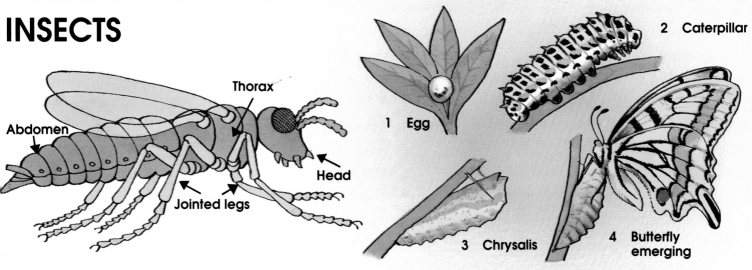

Abdomen

Thorax

Head

Jointed legs

1 Egg
2 Caterpillar
3 Chrysalis
4 Butterfly emerging

Insects are invertebrates, that is, they have their skeletons on the outside of their bodies. This exoskeleton is a hard covering with joints so that the insect can move easily.

Adult insects have six legs and three parts to their bodies — the head, thorax, and abdomen. Since they are cold-blooded, they cannot control their body heat and must rely on the temperature of their surroundings.

Some insects, such as butterflies and moths, go through metamorphosis, four stages of body development.

The female lays an egg that hatches into a caterpillar called a larva. When it is fully grown, the larva builds a hard case around its body, called a cocoon. At this stage the insect is called a pupa or chrysalis. Inside the case the pupa changes into its adult form and eventually emerges.

Fly's-eye view

Many adult insects have compound eyes. A compound eye is split up into lots of tiny hexagonal lenses, each one providing its own picture. The housefly shown above has about 4,000 lenses in each eye.

A compound eye does not see very clearly, but it is efficient at detecting sudden movements. Scientists think that insects see the color spectrum differently from humans.

ARACHNIDS

Spiders belong to a group of creatures called arachnids. They are not insects, although they have an exoskeleton.

Many spiders build webs to trap flying insects for food. The tropical orb weaver spiders spin webs up to nearly 19 feet (5.8 m) in circumference.

The largest spiders are the bird-eaters of South America, whose legs can span over ten inches (25 cm). Brazilian wandering spiders have the strongest venom. Their bites can kill humans unless they are quickly treated.

Orb spider

33

FISH

Fish are vertebrates, that is, they have backbones and skeletons inside their bodies. They are usually of a streamlined shape that makes swimming easier.

Although they live in water, fish need to breathe oxygen like all animals. They obtain it by gulping in mouthfuls of water and passing it through their gills, which act as lungs. Oxygen from the water enters the fish's blood and the waste water pumps out through slits behind the head.

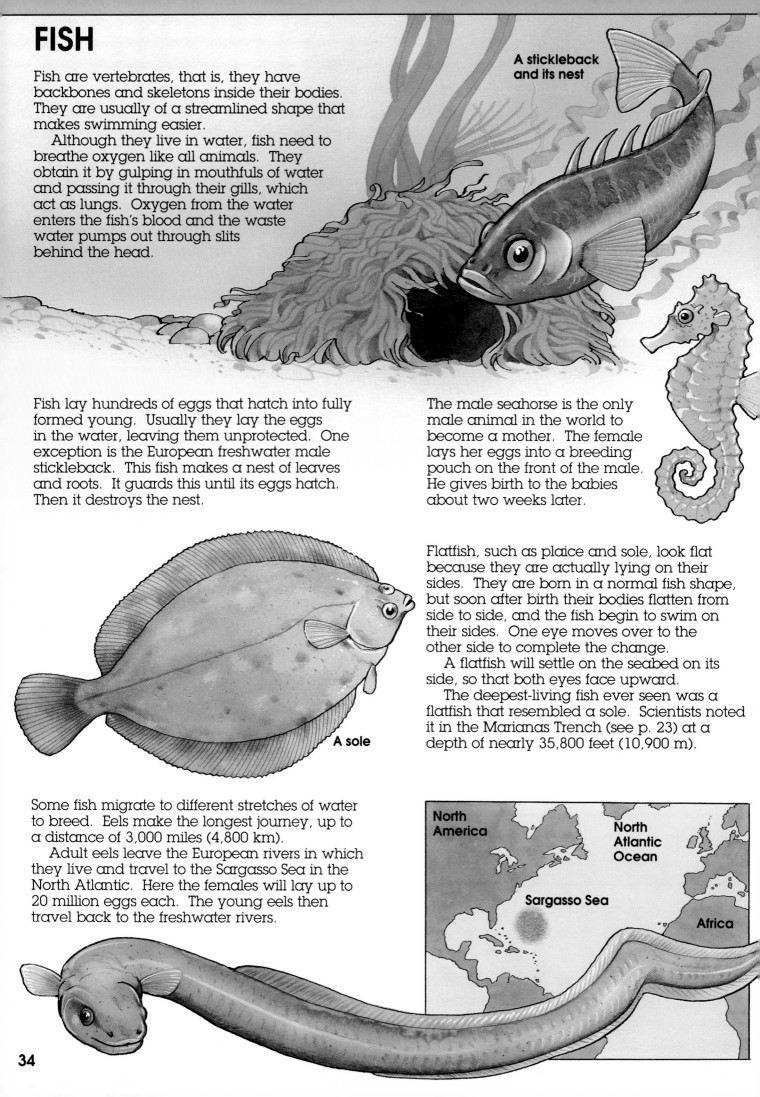

A stickleback and its nest

Fish lay hundreds of eggs that hatch into fully formed young. Usually they lay the eggs in the water, leaving them unprotected. One exception is the European freshwater male stickleback. This fish makes a nest of leaves and roots. It guards this until its eggs hatch. Then it destroys the nest.

The male seahorse is the only male animal in the world to become a mother. The female lays her eggs into a breeding pouch on the front of the male. He gives birth to the babies about two weeks later.

A sole

Flatfish, such as plaice and sole, look flat because they are actually lying on their sides. They are born in a normal fish shape, but soon after birth their bodies flatten from side to side, and the fish begin to swim on their sides. One eye moves over to the other side to complete the change.

A flatfish will settle on the seabed on its side, so that both eyes face upward.

The deepest-living fish ever seen was a flatfish that resembled a sole. Scientists noted it in the Marianas Trench (see p. 23) at a depth of nearly 35,800 feet (10,900 m).

Some fish migrate to different stretches of water to breed. Eels make the longest journey, up to a distance of 3,000 miles (4,800 km).

Adult eels leave the European rivers in which they live and travel to the Sargasso Sea in the North Atlantic. Here the females will lay up to 20 million eggs each. The young eels then travel back to the freshwater rivers.

North America

North Atlantic Ocean

Sargasso Sea

Africa

AMPHIBIANS

Amphibians can live both on water and on land. They are cold-blooded and most of them lay their eggs in water. These hatch into tadpoles with gills for breathing. Eventually they change into adults, growing legs and developing lungs for breathing on land.

The amphibian group includes frogs, toads, newts, and salamanders. Frogs and toads lay spawn that gradually develop, or metamorphose, into adult form.

Spawn

Tadpole stages

Frog

Metamorphosis

REPTILES

Reptiles, like amphibians, are cold-blooded. This means that they have to rely on their surroundings to keep their bodies at the right temperature so that they do not become too hot or too cold.

Crocodiles, alligators, lizards, tortoises, and snakes are all examples of reptiles.

The largest lizard is the huge Komodo monitor lizard from Indonesia. It looks like a dragon and can grow to over ten feet (3 m) long, weighing over 300 pounds (135 kg). This meat-eater has huge claws.

Komodo dragon

Many turtles live mostly under water but come on land to lay their eggs. The largest species is the Pacific leatherback turtle. Its shell can grow to over six feet (2 m) long.

Tortoises live on land. They are among the slowest-moving animals, averaging a speed of one-fourth mile (0.4 km) an hour.

Separate jawbones

Python

The reticulated python is the longest snake in the world and can take the largest mouthfuls of food. Its jaw is loosely hinged by ligaments, so it can open wide enough to swallow prey three times as wide as the snake itself!

35

BIRDS

Birds are warm-blooded vertebrates, which means that they can control their own body temperature. They all have beaks and wings, but not all birds can fly. The earliest known bird lived over 140 million years ago. It is called Archaeopteryx, and it resembled a reptile with a long tail.

Archaeopteryx

BIRD NESTS

Most birds build nests where they hatch their eggs and feed their young until the chicks are old enough to fly away. Nests can be built from all kinds of things, such as twigs, straw, mud, and sometimes even small pieces of rubbish left around by humans.

American bald eagles build huge nests of branches high up among cliffs. The nests can weigh over two tons. Eagles will keep these nests in use for as long as 70 years.

Bald eagle nest

Weaver birds build nests of straw up to 16 feet (5 m) wide in the treetops of Africa and Asia.

Up to 200 weaver birds may live in one nest, each family living in a separate chamber inside.

The female bower bird of Australia finds the color blue irresistible, so the male bird builds a nest using as many blue objects as possible, including flowers, cloth, and even bus tickets!

BIRD EGGS

A baby bird develops inside an egg, feeding on the yolk and white as it grows. Usually one parent bird sits on the egg to keep it warm, or incubate it.

Ostriches lay the biggest eggs, measuring up to eight inches (20 cm) high and six inches (15 cm) across. One would take about two hours to hard-boil, and it could feed 12 people.

Vervain hummingbirds of Jamaica lay the tiniest eggs, less than 0.4 inch (1 cm) long.

WINGS AND FEATHERS

Wing shapes depend on how birds feed and how they live. Birds of prey have large, broad wings so they can soar at high altitudes looking for food. A swift's narrow, pointed wings allow it to fly at up to 100 mph (160 kph) and turn quickly to catch flying insects. The largest individual wingspan, from a wandering albatross, was nearly 12 feet (3.6 m).

Feathers keep a bird's body warm and waterproof. The Japanese phoenix fowl, shown on the right, has tail feathers up to 35 feet (11 m) long!

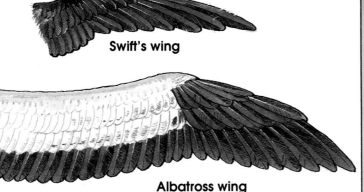

Bird of prey's wing

Swift's wing

Albatross wing

NONFLYING BIRDS

Some birds cannot fly, such as the ostrich, emu, and penguin. Penguins live mainly on fish and spend most of their time in the water, so their bodies are streamlined for swimming instead of flying. Like ducks, they have webbed feet that help them to paddle the water and swim more powerfully.

BIRD BEAKS

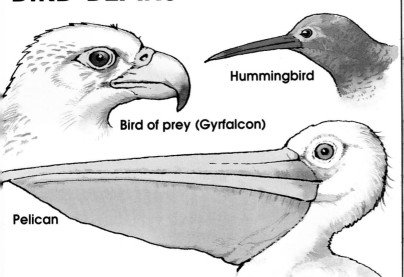

Hummingbird

Bird of prey (Gyrfalcon)

Pelican

Birds have different beaks depending on what they eat. For instance, hummingbirds have very long beaks so that they can feed on the nectar deep down inside flowers.

Pelicans live on fish, so the bottom part of a pelican beak forms a large skin pouch that can be used like a net to scoop fish out of the water.

MIGRATION

Arctic tern

Many birds migrate, flying from cold to warm places to spend the Winter or to breed. They return to their old homes in Spring or Summer. Arctic terns make an amazing trip of over 12,000 miles (19,200 km) between the Arctic and Antarctic.

MAMMALS

Mammals are warm-blooded vertebrates that feed their young milk. The world contains over 4,000 species of mammals. They can be divided into three groups — monotremes, marsupials, and placental mammals.

Kangaroo and baby

Duckbill platypus

The only monotremes are the duckbill platypus and the spiny anteater, both from Australia. They lay eggs and hatch their young.

Placental mammals include humans. The young are born fully developed, and they then live on milk until they can find food for themselves.

Marsupials, such as kangaroos and wombats, have tiny babies that crawl into a pouch on the mother's stomach where they slowly develop.

MAMMAL FEATURES

Mammals have adapted to living in many different parts of the world. In cold places most of them have thick fur. Some mammals, such as the ermine and the Arctic fox, have a brown coat in Summer and a white coat in Winter that camouflage them in snow.

Arctic fox

Camels

In very hot places, such as deserts, mammals have developed special traits to help them survive. For example, camels can go for many days without food or water. They use the fat in their humps for food and can drink up to 22 gallons (83 L) of water at once.

Some mammals have developed special features to make it easier for them to find food. For instance, the giraffe, the tallest mammal in the world, has a very long neck so that it can reach high up into trees to eat leaves and shoots. Giraffes can grow up to 18 feet (5.5 m).

Giraffes

FLYING MAMMALS

Bats are the only flying mammals, although some creatures in the group, such as flying squirrels and lemurs, can glide short distances.

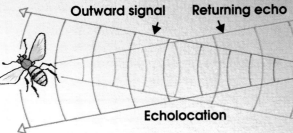

Outward signal   **Returning echo**

Echolocation

A bat's fingers are joined together by a thin membrane of skin stretched across them and attached to the back limbs to form a wing.

Bats are nocturnal creatures, that is, they rest during the day and are active at night when they hunt for food. In the dark, insect-eating bats find their prey and their way around by locating the echo of their high-pitched squeaking that humans can't hear.

The squeaking sounds strike any object in their path and the bats' large ears pick up the echo this makes. The bat can tell from this echo what direction to fly in to catch food or to avoid hitting trees and other things.

PRIMATES

The primate mammal group includes apes, monkeys, and humans. They are the most highly developed mammals, with large brains and hands that can grasp and manipulate objects. Apes and monkeys are intelligent creatures, and some have even been taught to communicate with humans by sign language.

Chimpanzees

SEA MAMMALS

There are about 120 species of sea mammals, including whales, dolphins, seals, walruses, and sea cows or dugongs. The blue whale is the biggest creature on the planet. It can grow up to 110 feet (34 m) long.

Instead of nostrils, whales and dolphins breathe through blowholes. Some dolphins can hold their breath for up to two hours, but all sea mammals need to surface regularly for air.

Killer whale

ANIMAL COLOR

Many animals use color as signals. For instance, they may use it to attract a mate or scare an enemy.

Among birds, the male usually wears the brightest plumage. For example, the male peacock has beautiful green and blue tail feathers, but the female peacock is a dull brown color.

When a male wants to attract a female, he dances in front of her, his tail feathers spread in a fan.

Male peacock

Female peahen

Many lizards can change the color of their skin to camouflage themselves against different backgrounds.

The chameleon's skin has special pigment cells in it containing green, yellow, or brown coloring. It can alter the size and shape of these cells to change to a color that best matches its background and hides it from enemies.

Chameleon

Animals such as tigers, tapirs, and zebras have distinctive striped coloring. While these stripes seem to be vivid and obvious, they actually provide a superb camouflage, blending in with long grass or jungle foliage.

There have been some rare cases of white tigers in India, but most tigers are fawn in color, with black or brown stripes.

ANIMAL FACT FINDER

Dinosaurs were gigantic animals that lived on Earth in a period lasting from 230 million to 65 million years ago.
The largest known dinosaur was the Seismosaurus. It measured over 100 feet (30 m) long, weighing at least 89 tons.

The giant squid is the largest invertebrate creature alive today. It grows up to 55 feet (17 m) long in some cases. Its eyes are the largest of any animal at over 15.5 inches (40 cm) across, about 16 times wider than a human eye.

The African goliath beetle is the heaviest insect in the world. It can weigh up to 3.5 ounces (100 g).
Giant stick insects from Indonesia grow the longest. The females of the species can reach a length of up to 13 inches (33 cm).

The saltwater crocodiles of South-east Asia, the largest reptiles, grow up to 28 feet (8.5 m), weighing up to two tons.
The smallest reptile ever seen was a gecko lizard only 1.4 inch (35 mm) long.

The biggest fish is the whale shark. It grows to nearly 42 feet (13 m) long.
The fish most dangerous to humans is the great white shark. This fierce creature has huge jaws with rows of very sharp teeth. It will often attack swimmers, mistaking them for fish.

The African ostrich is the largest bird in the world. It can grow up to 9 feet (2.7 m) tall and may weigh over 330 pounds (150 kg).
The smallest bird is the male bee hummingbird of Cuba. It is only about 2.25 inches (5.7 cm) long and weighs about 0.05 ounce (1.4 g). It feeds on flower nectar.

A newborn kangaroo, called a joey, is only about the size of a bumblebee. It gradually grows larger inside its mother's pouch.
Adult kangaroos have been known to leap over 30 feet (9 m) in one bound!

The most dangerous bat is the vampire bat, found in parts of South America. When it bites an animal or a human to feed on its blood, this bat may pass on rabies, a disease that can be fatal.

EARTH'S FUTURE

The Earth's natural resources continue to dwindle as they are quickly used up. Some areas also suffer industrial pollution. However, people are realizing the need to look after the natural world and conserve the countryside and its wildlife. In this section you can find out about some of the problems that need to be solved.

SAVING FORESTS

About 6% of the Earth's land surface is covered with hot, damp tropical rain forests. They contain nearly three-quarters of all the species of plants and animals in the world.

Each year large jungle areas are cut down for lumber or to clear space for building and farming. The destruction of these jungles could affect us all in the future because the world's temperature and rainfall patterns could be altered by the change.

WEATHER CHANGES

When wood, coal, and oil burn, they release carbon dioxide gas into the air. Many scientists worry that this could eventually form a screen that would stop excess heat from escaping the Earth, causing the temperature to rise.

Others theorize that pollution in the air could have the opposite effect, blocking out the Sun's rays and making the Earth colder.

When plants make food, they send water vapor into the air. The world's tropical jungles yield a large amount of vapor that joins the water cycle (see page 12) and eventually falls as rain. As more and more jungle is destroyed, less rain will fall, causing drought in many areas of the world.

THE OZONE LAYER

There is a layer of ozone gas 12 to 15 miles (19 to 24 km) above the Earth. It filters out the Sun's harmful ultraviolet rays.

Scientists think that the ozone layer can be partly destroyed from using aerosol sprays that contain the destructive gases of fluorocarbons. Some aerosols are now made without these fluorocarbons to try to solve this problem.

Ozone layer

Hole in layer

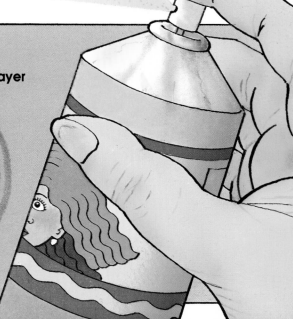

CONSERVING POWER

Gas, coal, and oil use is so high that scientists think we could run out in as little as 150 years. These so-called fossil fuels may be replaced by more lasting sources of power, such as the Sun.

In some regions, rooftop solar panels can be used to heat homes. The panels contain solar cells that gather the heat from the Sun's rays and convert it into electricity.

Scientists are finding ways to use the wind and sea to provide electricity.

Rooftop solar panels

SEAS AND RIVERS

The Earth's seas and rivers accumulate industrial waste pollution. This can lead to the death of many water creatures. For example, sea birds are often stranded on beaches with their wings and feathers coated with oil.

Many factories and power stations have installed filters that remove the poisonous chemicals from waste. Then sometimes they convert the harmless residue into fertilizers.

OVERFARMING

Clearing large areas to farm one crop can make land less fertile and eventually turn it into desert.

Today, farmers try to grow varieties of crops in their fields, and they replant trees and hedges to anchor the soil so it won't blow away.

Irrigation systems have reclaimed some of the world's desert land for growing crops.

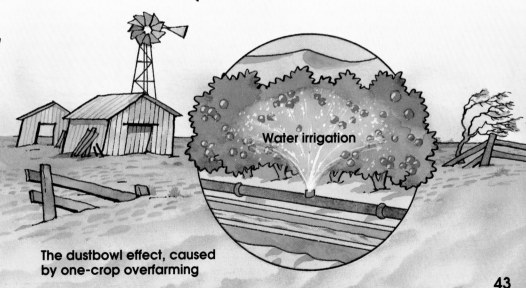

Water irrigation

The dustbowl effect, caused by one-crop overfarming

ANIMALS IN DANGER

About two-thirds of all the animal species in the world are endangered. This means that they could die out forever unless they are protected by law.

Humans hunt animals for their skins, fur, horns, and meat and for sport. Animals also die out if their homes undergo destruction.

A fifth of all the world's species of monkeys and apes is endangered. There are less than 400 mountain gorillas left in the wild today. These gentle giants live in the rain forests of Africa. Loggers cut down their trees, and poachers kill the gorillas themselves.

The golden lion marmoset is one of the rarest monkeys in the world. It inhabits the Brazilian rain forests. There are fewer than 200 of these marmosets now left in the wild.

Mountain gorillas

TREES AND PLANTS

About 40 million trees are cut down each year to make paper products alone. The increasing use of recycled paper will help conserve trees.

Plant species may die out if their habitat suffers ruin or if livestock overgrazes the land they grow on. Some rare plants now survive in conservation areas that are not farmed.

Some of the rarest plant species in the world are now known only from one wild specimen. In these cases, experts take cuttings to grow in botanical gardens so the plant won't die out.

SAVING THE NATURAL WORLD

Today there are many conservation groups helping to protect the Earth and its endangered plants and animals. Some have set up projects to help save rare creatures, such as pandas.

Zoos also help by breeding endangered creatures and reintroducing them to the wild.

Some groups replant trees and hedges or clean up seas and rivers.

CONSERVATION FACT FINDER

One of the rarest and most threatened species of bird is the ooaa of Hawaii. In 1980 only one pair of birds still survived in the wild.

To save the California condors from extinction, experts trapped one of the last two specimens living in the wild for use in breeding these birds in captivity. Fewer than 30 of these birds remain in the world.

The world's most threatened forests are the tropical rain forests found in places such as South America.

Each year developers cut down an area of rain forest about the size of Switzerland. Experts say that by the beginning of the next century about a third of all the rain forests in the world will have been destroyed. There is no way to replant or replace rain forest.

The Mediterranean Sea, between Europe and Africa, is one of the most polluted stretches of water found anywhere in the world.

Oil spilled from tankers has formed a thin film over parts of the sea. Sewage pollutes some coastal areas, making them unsafe for humans to swim in.

An animal is officially extinct if no one has sighted it for over 50 years. The thylacine, or Tasmanian wolf, is the world's rarest marsupial. The last thylacine held in captivity died in 1936. Nearly forty-four years later, in 1982, a wildlife ranger reported seeing a single thylacine in the wild. There have been no other proven sightings since.

Some plants considered extinct reappear growing in a very small area. One of the rarest trees is called *Pennantia baylisiana*. A single female tree grew in New Zealand in 1945. One of the rarest flowers is the lady's slipper orchid. One single flower flourished in May 1983.

The rarest sea mammal is the Longman's beaked whale. The last recording of the species was a skull found in 1955.

Another rare sea animal is the Atlantic ridley turtle of Mexico. The female turtles come ashore to lay their eggs in sand, but people often robbed their nests for food. The turtles now have a protected nesting beach guarded by armed soldiers.

The Bali tiger is the rarest big cat and one of the world's rarest land animals. Until the end of the last century the species was quite common. But hunters killed so many that in 1963 experts thought only three or four remained.

The species apparently died out in 1973, but in 1979 scientists found claw marks on a tree trunk that one of the tigers could have made.

FOR MORE INFORMATION

MAGAZINES

Here are some children's magazines that have had recent articles about the natural world, and its weather, oceans, plants, and animals. Look for them at your library, or write to the publishers listed below for information about subscribing.

Current Science
Field Publications
4343 Equity Drive
Columbus, OH 43228

National Geographic World
National Geographic Society
P.O. Box 2330
Washington, DC 20013-9865

Ranger Rick
National Wildlife Federation
8925 Leesburg Pike
Vienna, VA 22184-0001

Dolphin Log
Cousteau Society Membership
930 West 21st Street
Norfolk, VA 23517

Owl
P.O. Box 11314
Des Moines, IA 50340

Science World
P.O. Box 644
Lyndhurst, NJ 07071-9985

ADDRESSES

The organizations listed below have information about plants and animals and other aspects of the natural world. When you write to them, tell them exactly what you want to know. Be sure to include your full name, age, and address.

National Audubon Society
950 Third Avenue
New York, NY 10022

Pacific Forestry Center
506 W. Burnside Road
Victoria, BC
Canada   V8Z 1M5

Sierra Club
730 Polk Street
San Francisco, CA 94109

BOOKS

The following books will give you more information about plant and animal life and different environments of the natural world. Look for them in your library, or ask someone to order them for you at a bookstore.

All About Deserts. Sanders (Troll)
Amazing World of Animals. Jefferies (Troll)
Amazing World of Plants. Marcus (Troll)
Animals of the Tropical Forests. Johnson (Lerner)
Arctic and Antarctic Regions. Sabin (Troll)
Birds. Morris (Raintree)
A Closer Look at Reptiles. Pope (Franklin Watts)
Deserts. Wilkes (EDC)
Earth Afire! Volcanoes and Their Activity. Fodor (Morrow)
Environment. Cook (Crown)
Favorite Wild Animals of North America. Vandivert (Scholastic)
Fish. Sutton (Wonder)
Forests and Jungles. Bains (Troll)
Geology. Boyer (Hubbard Scientific)
Glaciers and Ice Caps. Bramwell (Franklin Watts)
Insects. Horton (Franklin Watts)
Mountains and Earth Movements. Bain (Franklin Watts)
Mysteries and Marvels of Insect Life. Owen (EDC)
Ocean Life. Cook (Crown)
Plants and Flowers. Holley (Penworthy)
Rescue from Extinction. Brown (Dodd)
Rivers and Lakes. Mulherin (Franklin Watts)
Small World of Birds. Pluckrose, editor (Franklin Watts)
Tropical Rain Forests. Goetz (Morrow)
Weather Watch. Ford (Lothrop, Lee & Shepard)
Wild Animals. Keen (Wonder)
World of Weather. Adler (Troll)
The World's Oceans. Sandok (Franklin Watts)

GLOSSARY

Acid rain
Rain with a high concentration of acids; caused by atmospheric water forming acids when passing through air that contains sulfur dioxide, nitrogen oxide, and similar products that come from burning coal or oil; acid rain destroys plant and animal life, pollutes waterways, and erodes buildings and other constructed objects.

Cold-blooded
Unable to generate the body's own heat; the body temperature is like that of the surrounding air, land, or water; in some animals, changing temperatures forces them to seek different, more suitable surroundings; all animals are cold-blooded except birds and mammals.

Cordillera
A system or chain of mountains, especially the principal mountain range of a continent or a similarly extensive undersea mountain chain.

Ice Age
The latest period of extensive glaciation that began almost two million years ago and ended 10,000 years ago; the glaciers expanded and melted back many times during this period; in the Western Hemisphere during this time, ice covered the present-day northern United States, Greenland, and Canada.

Invertebrate
Any animal without a backbone; any animal not a fish, amphibian, reptile, bird, or mammal.

Lemur
A small tree-dwelling primate with large eyes, a long tail, a pointed muzzle, and soft, woolly fur; found in the African and Asian tropics.

Malaria
A disease of tropical and subtropical areas, caused by a single-celled parasite of red blood cells, transmitted through the bite of an infected mosquito; the infected person suffers cycles of chills and fevers.

Marsupial
An order of mammals that have an external abdominal pouch containing the mammaries, or milk glands; the newborn crawls into the mother's pouch to nurse there for several months; includes the kangaroo, bandicoot, opossum, and wombat.

Monotremes
Any of the lowest order of mammals that lay eggs and have a single opening for the digestive and urinary tracts and for the reproductive organs; includes the duckbill platypus and the spiny anteater.

Ozone
A form of oxygen consisting of three atoms in each molecule instead of the two atoms in normal oxygen; plants produce oxygen that enters the atmosphere and at high altitudes is changed into ozone by the action of the Sun's ultraviolet rays; ozone protects the Earth's surface from harmful ultraviolet rays.

Parasitic
Living on another, as a plant or animal that lives on or in an organism of another species from which it derives nourishment or protection without benefiting the host and often harming it.

Placental mammals
Mammals that develop an internal placenta, or blood-rich organ, through which the developing young are nourished and their wastes are removed until birth, when it leaves the mother's body along with the newborn; most mammals are placental mammals.

Rain forest
A dense, evergreen forest occupying a tropical region having abundant rainfall throughout the year; the rain forests of the world produce a significant amount of the atmosphere's oxygen while using up large amounts of carbon dioxide; destruction of rain forest may result in less oxygen, less ozone, and excess carbon dioxide that may raise the temperature of the Earth's surface; such higher temperatures would be harmful to crops, animals, and people.

Sargasso Sea
A two-million-square mile (five-million-sq km) region of calm water in the North Atlantic between the West Indies and the Azores; this body of water rotates, dragged around by a system of ocean currents; it consists of a warm-water layer about 3,000 feet (1,000 m) deep that rides on top of the cold water below; it is well known for its abundance of a seaweed with long floating fronds; though harboring some shrimp, crabs, mollusks, and a few small fish, the region is not as rich in life as other ocean areas.

Thorax
The middle of the three exoskeleton-covered segments of an insect's body, it supports the insect's three pairs of legs and its wings; the other insect parts are the head and abdomen; in spiders, the thorax and head form one structure.

Vertebrate
Any animal with a backbone; vertebrates have other bony supports that together make up the internal skeleton; vertebrates include fish, amphibians, reptiles, birds, and mammals.

Warm-blooded
Possessing the ability to generate one's own body heat; the body temperature is more or less constant; it is independent of and usually higher than the surrounding temperature; only birds and mammals are warm-blooded; some scientists think that many of the dinosaurs might also have been warm-blooded.

INDEX